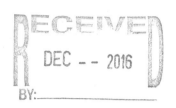
OCULAR PROOF

OCULAR PROOF

MARTHA RONK

OMNIDAWN PUBLISHING
OAKLAND, CALIFORNIA
2016

Cover art © *Shadow of Sign*, Christina Niazian

Cover and Interior fonts: Adobe Caslon Pro and Adobe Jensen Pro

Cover and interior design by Cassandra Smith

Offset printed in the United States
by Edwards Brothers Malloy, Ann Arbor, Michigan
On 55# Glatfelter B18 Antique
Acid Free Archival Quality Recycled Paper

Library of Congress Cataloging-in-Publication Data

Names: Ronk, Martha Clare, author.
Title: Ocular proof / Martha Ronk.
Description: Richmond, California : Omnidawn Publishing, 2016.
Identifiers: LCCN 2016017043 | ISBN 9781632430250 (paperback : alk. paper)
Classification: LCC PS3568.O574 A6 2016 | DDC 811/.54--dc23
LC record available at https://lccn.loc.gov/2016017043

Published by Omnidawn Publishing, Oakland, California
www.omnidawn.com (510) 237-5472 (800) 792-4957
10 9 8 7 6 5 4 3 2 1
ISBN: 978-1-63243-025-0

This book is for Jacob Lifson and Hannah Lifson and in memory of their father, Ben Lifson.

1.
PHOTOGRAPHS

A blurry photograph

The tree azalea overwhelms evening with its scent,
defining everything and the endless fields.

Walking away, suddenly, it slices off and is gone.

The visible object blurs open in front of you,
the outline of a branch folds back into itself, then clarifies—just as you
        turn away—

and the glass hardens into glass

as you go about taking care of things abstractedly
one thing shelved after another, as if they were already in the past,

needing nothing from you until, smashing itself on the tile floor,
the present cracks open the aftermath of itself.

Paris 1926 Atget

Photography born in an inaugural mist—
                              Atget getting it by not getting it
in the flare behind plane trees, in the street lamp's dot of light
that could be anything, but it's the *Quay d'Anjou* not an error in printing.
To say it's actual light isn't it either
or an actual tree or what sort of tree and could one walk over and touch it

  —in that twilight zone between seeing and not seeing—

men on the street blurring their shirt fronts and pulling a cart
blown by wind and emulsion past the door of the corner building,
Cognac, Rhum and Kirsch where a man in stone is fixing a stone shoe.
It all counts for more than it is—more of what light and wind
and Paris are in the exact year it was.

 The fog which obscures the beginnings of photography is not quite as thick
 as that which envelops the beginnings of printing. Perhaps more discernible for
 photography was the fact that many had perceived that the hour for the invention
 had come.
  Walter Benjamin

Take #2

Does staring into the black and white contours of a photo
enable a rapprochement with the unreality of one's own life,
a way to see peculiarity as a back staircase in an old house in a city
so memorably far, dark but navigable, the stairs lacking undulation,
items strewn across a landscape, fixed and determined,
the borders of history and frame set and watching her feet going up and down,
counting the risers that are always 16 despite the deformations of dreams,
always scuffed and smelling of dust, the taste of a local architect
influenced by city regulations and his sense of propriety and then turning
the page to an image of the purported documents of an ordinary scene,
a few weeds wavering in the foreground and the jagged outlines against a sky,
a 7pm time of day, summer, a particular dry rush of air,
and a cutout of one's own days called up, and the inability to get at
the unlocatable bereavement left on the stairs to be carried up when you go.

Ghosts

That blur in the corner of the photograph
      in the hills which fold over on themselves in infinite regress
            when witnesses are looking elsewhere

On the blue steps a child made her way slowly and with specific intent

Kertész photographed stairs extending past the small figure and out of sight

In ghost photos, the see-through specters stand behind the bereaved—
      they saw it, they believed—a beloved walking in from the other world

In the hours spent on the blue stairs pages came alive and there was no time
      until interrupted

Baudelaire worried lest photography *impinge on the sphere of the intangible*
      and imaginary

> *In the late 1850s Gustave Le Gray pioneered a way of combining two negatives*
> *to create a print that showed a magical combination of sea or land and sky that*
> *had, in fact, never existed, hoping to evoke the visceral emotion of* Wuthering
> Heights.
>   Geoff Dyer

The picture plane

The actual world pushes a shrub of Ceanothus, stained of its purple,
up against the picture plane, a messy splay of branches,
as though missing all the cues it moved in close, breathing stale air.
Some child has put sticky fingers in your hair, is sitting on the edge of your coat,
is the child whose awkward stance is your own shoes
pointing pigeon-toed in a photograph you remember the awkward itch of.
Also called California lilac, the plant thrives on neglect, the imperfect conditions
of hot wind sweeping across deserts in a movie of so much violence
the children live on it, sensing a breakdown that's already occurred,
their games dwarfed by a range of San Gabriel mountains
almost indistinguishable and only seemingly benign.

No Sky (after Robert Adams's *California: Views*)

No sky a gray backdrop merely
and below: the scraggle of dusty fronds, the scrub oak and scrub jay
whose abrasive noises sharpen in response.

Shadows proliferate in deep furrows no sky above
merely a scrim registering conical thrusts, a heightened flurry &
outlines of branches, the dead ones slowly petering out.

magnificent ruin   the cut through the field   blasted chaparral

As I understand my job, it is, while suggesting order, to make things appear as much as possible to be the way they are in normal vision.

An unvoiced series of sentences, without articulation,
with gray shapes, formulating a syntax loosening and then tightening from
edge to edge.

The frame sets a border down from which a thin straggle hangs at random
like purposeful intrusion, and so unlike

and the interstate (in the title) missing from the photograph itself
merely a dry riverbed, the density of shadows trapped in the confusion
of bush and bush-like tree

except from higher up than the rest, its thin trunk arched against
no sky

colorless, less often remarked upon, appositely emotionless these days,
a relic, like the fan palm living at the edges of water.

THE PHOTOGRAPHIC OBJECT

It's too close or too far to be seen at the fogged horizon,
      my balance is off, clearing away the brush at the side of the photograph,

      tying up bundles to be carted away, and pruning what's left.

                          What for god's sake
is that roundish bit on top of a shrub over there,
branches any good wind might break,
              asymmetry in disheveled light—

it's either dense shadow or a tree, either downhill or a camera tilt,
ironic
        or a story hidden in what's seen.

What was I seeing in the dusty leaves and skin and endless hours,
      even afterwards (calm, astringent)
           in the still black and white.

*It frequently happens, moreover—and this is one of the charms of photography—
that the operator himself discovers on examination, perhaps long afterwards, that he
has depicted many things he had no notion of at the time.*
Walter Benjamin, "A Short History of Photography"

Brassai's night photos

Photographing Paris at night, Brassai wanted to be raised

to the level of object: *the world is richer than I,*

the wall speaking to him in graffiti chipped from a childish drawing

of interlocking hearts only seeming symbolic, only seeming impossible.

On such days reification attracts as the whole city spreads out before you,

metempsychosis not from flesh to flesh, but (from where he stood

his large camera before him) into bridges across the Seine.

> *Ultimately, Photography is subversive not when it frightens, repels, or even stigmatizes, but when it is pensive, when it thinks.*
> Roland Barthes

Legs

After the moment of the take,

the street walker's legs stretch out in black stockings
towards some unknown—

                                      a stranger perhaps, a future down which
light provides the time in which streetlamps become the ordinary light of morning

                                      a lift of her foot, the white gap between shoe
and shadow an imprint of tenderness, wet from the rain,

one foot following the other as walking becomes what she is
but for the momentary

                                  photo of the not-yet, the wait-a-moment,
the what-else-might-there-have been—

OF SOMEWHERE OUT WEST (*Robert Adams*)

The photograph drags on in its washed-out way and the sky's missing
        behind the usual white of western light.

Tire marks whiten the dirt, disappear in the puddle left from last night's rain
        the white isn't white, the black isn't black,
                but more incremental shades of gray than seems possible.

Some verticals called trees are on a small rise in the distance.

It's not a wasteland by either metaphor or fact.

Ideals haven't settled in (nor a crescent moon, nor a gibbous)
        but off-frame a lament seems about to begin, to hold off.

as the ordinariness of human effort claims its own—
        tire marks laid down by the absent track hauling stuff

and we're drawn in as witnesses to the material facts
        of having been there, the insistent weight of being.

ELEGY (AND A PHOTOGRAPH BY ROBERT ADAMS)

Headlights light up a weed, then a cone of blossoms lifting off into shadows
driven by the demarcation of time
and they stay with us as we go forward in undifferentiated dark.

Part of the trouble is an echo of objects just past and those about to arrive.

They fade out slowly
those conical bright shapes out from the field and across the dashboard.

He had walked into/fallen into the truck crossing the road.
Later he had fallen into the water near the pier.
Earlier he had decided or he hadn't decided or it had shaped itself around him.

It's hard to see sunflowers in the dark but the dark center surrounded
by many gray petals is immediately clear, despite shadows,
despite tricks played on the eye.

It seems more than obvious that nothing particular is about to happen.

When the painters paint the white line down the middle of the road do they
see how it shines in the near dark nearly upon us.

*Now, everywhere, in the street, the café, I see each individual under the aspect of
ineluctably having-to-die, which is exactly what it means to be mortal.—And no less
obviously, I see them as not knowing this to be so.*
Roland Barthes

Intimate Portraits

In the photograph of a rather upright and formal black and white
the queen, looking like a Giacometti, turns to look over her shoulder.

One hand crosses over the other so that in the background
it could pass for an extension of his hand,

a marriage portrait of sorts, they wear the correct corsages
seated as they are in a circle of light.

I've left it where you left it and yet the circles of dust betray,
as did the strand of hair in the Japanese diary, a lure of sorts,

a tantalizing effect, an arcane method to gain sexual control
over which compliance also plays its part

and the confession of being without a language
by which to indicate a changed position

of what should go here, what should go there, for which
I'd wear anything for the next portrait you have in mind.

Taped to the refrigerator

The artificial memory of where one hasn't been
shows up in a photo with triangular roofs and customarily

taped to the refrigerator (in flannels and gutta-percha things)
imbued with the textures of the recognizable and looking down

from the window on the truck parked side-ways in the street
mercury water sliding down the gutter in the dust,

lit by a long exposure, the technical dimension of which is
as clearly remembered as wet fingers dipped in the gutter after a long rain

sleepwalking rooms where the concept of shapes calls up
something deep enough to evoke the familiar in its unfamiliarity,

on the verge of driving off, blurrily and distantly edged
colors smudged beyond belief, coming into their blue.

*For it is another nature that speaks to the camera than to the eye: other in
the sense that a space informed by human consciousness gives way to a space
informed by the unconscious.*
Walter Benjamin, "A Short History of Photography"

A Kirlian effect—ghosts

Of course they aren't around anymore they never were in that way
nor at the time and it's hard to grasp how ghostly
it is behind the printed record and whether new forms of being
are generated is a question arising in consequence

proliferation giving even less ground to stand on and suggesting
an obsession with whoever looks *out* not *in* on the world
slowly lifting its waters around and unable to maintain its shape.

No one was close to dying in that photograph—all the lights were on

in the glow of the evening and only distance prevented knowing
down to the patterns on the wall and the rummaging around.
In the sky all the stars that aren't there are almost visible to children
waiting around, excited to a pitch when one goes suddenly out.

A PHOTOGRAPH OF A SIDE WINDOW

Dusty leaves patterning the siding with shadows,
open half-way for air on what must be a summer night,
an eternal return located in its technical reproducibility,
time repeating its grasses and the feeling of grass,
moving forward as walking across to get to the window
and seeing oneself in the glass reflection by chance
and wondering how she got out of the place she's usually in,
the past most frequently, given the fear of the photograph
propped on the bureau where she and the others served cups
from the momentous tablecloth spread corner to corner
at a 40 degree angle to the side of the house
as the day faded in the original of which this is only a copy
calling up what never was in the tonal variations of gray
as the house is only a copy of *house* writ large, exposed
as the flesh and bone, coats and jackets of the lived again.

Before leaving

The nighttime lingers over the balcony taking me up inside a yellow bureau
with drawers.

        Tendrils coil and the colors mistakenly water the plants morphing
wrists and ankle bones. A young bird zigzags the path a few feet in front,

unsteady traces in the gravel,

yet slows when I do. Things seem missing when I wake and an artificial brightness
steals the sky.

        The unattainable we just call what's left over
or what's to come.

        Waiting to leave I watch her photograph an unknown plant.

Primula sinensis—remembering beforehand,   a flash of white.

*[My book] speaks only of ghost images, images that have not yet issued, or rather, of latent
images, images that are so intimate that they become invisible.*
        Hervé Guibert

The familiar/unfamiliar

If executed with care, forward and back might elicit a structure
in which coming to know her could take place along the mobius strip
of withdrawal, backstepping into the original position
                    without its usual trappings of aura and awe

yet nevertheless and at once something luminous and familiar
as the girl reached down so many sandals ago and carved herself into memory
as one reads of Kafka and his mother
                    staring into one another's eyes

as all assumptions falter and one face appears identical to the other
and comes to be by approaching a state of profound stillness
                    enabling someone, almost anyone, to adopt similar features.

A photograph arrives and seems endlessly intriguing
but sent off too quickly to the wrong viewer
                    puzzling over an intimacy that never was.

the photograph is the advent of myself as another
Roland Barthes

Sugimoto's seas

A vertiginous quality equivalent to the movement of waters
(despite the stillness of the photograph) overtakes the surfaces
although the idea of repetition has been altered by the relation
of foreground to background, a viewer so fragile as to be a mere mark,
distant, overly iconographic, such that *I am looking at or staring out at*
repositions whatever point of view is meant to color what is seen
as the opacity of surface blocks all but the most jittery of questions
despite the urgency, despite the beauty impenetrable in every direction
as the density and opacity of the sea stymies all human endeavor
ever mesmerized by its own iteration and disturbingly lit.

SUGIMOTO BY THE SEA

1.
English Channel, Weston Cliff 1994

striations of seaweed   pushing at the surface
darker water at the lower edge
        orientation by a long horizon
a frame split in two by the shadings of gray and an all-
encompassing murky float—
                    obliteration of position

2.
Tyrrhenian Sea, Corsica, 1994

as if ridges formed the way fingers feel

                        dragged across the surface

liquid solidified

the skin of surface transformed into wood grain
                and each age through which it passed,
as if tactile could be rubbed into being

                by mere shadow

3.
Celtic Sea, Boscastle, 1994

mist is mist only as rescued by light
                                sculpting a shape out of shadow
hissing itself as steam in a sick room, breathing into
                                a loopy curve of white on a curve of
dark
a graphic shape rotating itself
                                a profile turning slowly forward.

Mortified

We're objectified, reified and will be here the way we have always been
by the power of being mortified, the mortifying moment lopsidedly morphing,
coalescing, certifying the corpse is alive, *as corpse*
and showing up in imposition—the posed tilt with the frozen smile,
the allegorical moment, quintessential child, rendered by subtraction,
without the climbing, the oak, the scratched-up skin and myopic eyes,
flailing limbs in an unending game of twirl and scoff, hems and leaps
lost in the click of petrifaction—closed up inside the little box.

*[Photography] creates sudden death...the camera's click suspends life in an act that
the developed film reveals as its essence.*
              Pierre Mac Orlan

Self-portraits with mirror: Florence Henri 1893-1982

Of a doorway, of a mirror, of a repeated repetition
     of the intensity of doubled stares,

the flushed face, taut skin reflected off the surface

geometric poses and capers brought to a standstill
     the "optical unconscious" lodged in mirrored flaws,

records of how often we have to see ourselves

projected and gallantly posed
     dramatized and droll, chin in a V of hands,

an artifice of mouths, the erotic claustrophobia of space,

light off the silver balls, off the silver mirror, off everywhere windows and doors,
     off my face—I make it
          —the shadow and light obey my will and say

     what I want them to say.

Kertesz's photograph of Martinique

A shadow outlined on the other side of frosted glass
offers a narrative amorphous clouds and indeterminate sea resist
as the sky lifts or darkens in its upper reaches
in response to the sea forming a triangle with the fence line
and the leaning figure, hunched forward—
can't see out, can't see in, rapt in what view he has
angled in relation to what draws us both, the obvious sea and sky—
it could be murky given the frosted glass placed to his side, yet
not *melancholy*, too sickly and dramatic a word—
although Kertesz himself used it for his tulip drooping
lower than the base of the vase, a severe gravitational force.

2.
INFORMATION SYSTEMS

Rapture

Into this file must go the viewing of films so that characters leave one room
and enter another in which events happen to them in the dark.
History comes to a head in the time of the disaster that structures it.
It depends on knowing that raptor and rapture share the same root.
The hawk over the cleft in the hill heading towards its prey heading towards
where the wind is taking it. Bill Evans in a nightclub I never went to.
Documentaries must be filmed in grainy black and white
and it's best to include voice-overs to explain the inscrutable parts.
Even a nightclub is an historical event given the costumes women wore
and Lauren Bacall gambling too much and rhapsodic about him or acting the part.
I pretend to look at the hawk and it seems a good idea given the circumstances
so I make myself do it and after a time it is all I want to do all afternoon.

An illegible day

It was a highly illegible day
plants ramped up in a waltz, loud and whirly,
outdoor irony being mastered and dimmed
though you'd think it'd be otherwise given the verbal cues.
These are examples mostly missing from philosophical discourse
and always when most needed since otherwise how's even the fact of reading
to be understood and other cultures, and *my time of day*
playing its lovelorn and loveladen tune.
It was that sort of day, my immersion in voices
more than amplitude, more than nasturtium hanging colors
across the usual path. I'm mostly getting it wrong here as usual,
still, whatever it is out there I want it:
a day of a monumental size,
yellow-green on the Rubina and behind the shuttered eye
hazards and guesses, the bright and unprintable.

Remembering beforehand

If what's out of reach is, then words step in, rhetorically or
otherwise, and if they won't, then perhaps some vagaries—
an illegible hand, the camel clouds, or vastnesses waiting to sound.
"I promise" becoming a determinant despite evidence or so-called
knowledge, and any effort at the follow-through so weak
that leaving out a comma or two brings one down,
fosters the inability to locate the necessary accoutrements.
Such a small glass of tea, such elaborate etchings on the Persian glass,
such hopefulness in—what did he call it—the table of memory.
Each utterance a re-write, yet the only pathway to articulation
a tale recited in order to avoid what I know I know.

Information systems

Digitally speaking marked up our walls and placed before us
the necessity of filling the screens better left unsaid
those ugly things passing through the mind
in the utter depths of night one might have let loose before
the BBC fills in with the breakdown of notorious shapes.
We say the image of some sidelong glance fades as language itself
into 19th century novels now cut down to size and rendered as harmless
as plots without the history of whaling or the thoughts of a minor character
who didn't have friends in every city nor much sense of geography
or music itself fading from view in the classical ways of overgrown ruin
as impatience overtakes the best of motives on the best of days
when the filter systems are all down and whatever leaks through
is a break in the assignation, a gift as it were necessarily dependent
on random chance and the Cagean notes, single, percussive, pure.

EVIDENTIARY

The evidence of something, some alarm clock, some fraying,
clings. We cling to it.

Even photoshopped or cropped. Or some ineptitude has crept in.

Where is it that it stops and something else begins and if the clock
falls on its side and it slips and you're at the side of me unless you're not

it's noon in consequence,

The picture I saw was formed before the alarm, before even
we met and if there's a stereogram of the picturesque,
it's even more so.

All this mere happenstance mapped onto some arrow headed straight
at the future, still it's embarrassing how randomly all is placed.

Still, there's the imposition of some arrangement, some way in which,
despite changing nature, things seem to have happened for a reason—

        something fiercer perhaps from another era
or they couldn't help it as we can't ours—

        Mozart's opera in its rising crescendo, doors flung open wide.

Our lived experience

Boxed-up illusions lure a crowd of the tee-shirted,
well-fed, under blue-rays promising another rush of adrenalin
straight to the heart, loins, finger-tips bright with today's polish,
blue-based, magenta, scarlet, and ice red,
despite cold weather perfect for squirreling inside
collecting as many references as possible
before the after-days meld into days more recognizable.
Catastrophes proliferate in snappable containers
under the arm, in the bag, stuck in a variety of knapsacks
according a kind of control absent from the somewhat
larger world one reads aloud in the newspaper.
Knowing is out of the question given the need to pursue
flashable reproductions of the same, and
given *the posthumous character of our lived experience.*

(Walter Benjamin)

Filmic history

Tracking what one actually thinks is more than
I'll take a walk, more than keeping verbs from sliding into other verbs
as the museum corridors fan open, history presses in,
waltzers waltz and Anastasia ballets her way along,
Danae receives her showers of gold.
Everyone seems surprised to be speaking Russian but they do,
and the gilt doors continue to open as the years go by.
When the portrait of Rembrandt as himself appears,
disguised as X in a velvet toque, the naked women move
aside for an era closer to our own.
Its rapidity, the room of revolution and boxes of pine,
the collapsing drywall so like Siberian snow,
the sounds that come from somewhere else endlessly far away
keep interrupting what it is one thinks
and the times one lives in that are never quite one's own.

OCULAR PROOF

Be sure of it, give me the ocular proof.
Othello

Dangling itself Lissitzky-like and tantalizing
and commonly regarded as a path to knowledge (*videlicet*),
still it's all dependent on shocks to the system,
that node radiating up and down the spinal column
(in the days when the skeleton seemed nearly benign),
and balance, a quality assigned in a classical sense to art;
thus the associated moments in tantalizing array,
the connective tissue that becomes the ocular proof to trick us,
colored candy in seductive shades, the erotic charge
which proves the case and one's own idea of it—
how to explain to anyone the simple *frisson*
and how trace that back to anything but tracing, *Mon Frère*,
to a drama in which rhetorical proof was viewed as absolute.

The voice must belong to someone
(from *The Unnamable*, Samuel Beckett)

The repetitions bring forth the usual phrases useful for daylight,
cross-stitched rhetoric and the talking that gamely takes up
national debt, carbon trades and reasons for going on best confronted by going on.

When the voice fails (does it alone convince us, walking along, talking
to ourselves, naming the varied birds in the field and clouds taking up the usual space)
silence stares us in the face and breathing is what's advised to fool the brain
into another day.

But leaving that aside, take the voice so marshaled by syntax,
the present progressive and dangling participles and it must belong to someone,
an argument that takes us to the inward voicings hard-wired to the unnamable
out of which one hears things, stirring things, evocative things,
things that with practice might suffice.

The voice must belong to someone, we say,
hoping for some homunculus who stirs about among the organs,
a recognizable sort who will wish for things and take them up,
meditate into a kind of long-admired sturdiness, someone, say someone.

INDEXICALITY

Be the first to like this photograph, stand next to it and grin,
don't vacate your face, be utterly present, wear suitable clothes,
morph and take the next available pose,
never mind the metallica, the highstepping march and flag
keep it up *mit macht* and roll to the comfortable side of the bed near the door.
Who snapped the one with the lifted brows and meringue spun hair,
you do like it, don't you, at least up close, but close the fucking door
before the breezes take over the cold shoulder, before dinner and lunch,
and lest the dress slip down a notch or two turn the neck to the side
closest to daylight: a good shot, a good likeness,
a goodness recorded in the dewy pores of *quote/unquote* alabaster skin
glowing to the music of sliding violins, a background accompaniment
to fingerprints, coffeestains, marks you've tried to make on the world
proofs of existence in initials scratched into the mirrored door.

ILLEGIBILITY

Complete strangers rise up and speak
in complete paragraphs with crisp consonants and highly elaborated syntax
taking as long as they want and if the exchange halts for days or weeks
there's time enough to straighten up or reconsider posture and frequently
one simply abandons the scene leaving perfectly articulated gestures
hanging in mid air in order to pursue a counter line of thought or twist it

into circumstances requiring attention from more than one angle.
Often as well—
and this is more acute over time—it isn't that illegibility
predominates as that the multitude blurs the edges
as in *sfumato* or even—although this happens less frequently—
overlaps them, so that deciphering unzips the *doublement*
and one's left a bit stranger.

3.
SHADOWS AND ELEGIES

The most transitory of things, a shadow, the proverbial emblem of all that is fleeting and momentary, may be fettered by the spells of our 'natural magic,' and may be fixed for ever in the position which it seemed only destined for a single instant to occupy....
Fox Talbot

That the photograph is always touched by death means that it offers us a glimpse of a history to which we no longer belong.
Siegfried Kracauer

In praise of shadows

Shaping even the word with its left-over sense of the sea-cove,
waves lapping, an architectural and elaborate series of masts.

Al-kubba, the vault.

In early churches built over the tombs of martyrs, the darkness is suffocating
as it slides across the walls.

Drawn to cryptography Poe may himself have published the challenge
under a *nom de plume* cementing his reputation among the cognoscenti

or it may be a metaphor for the genetic code.

In his Goldberg variations Bach often imbedded numbers
mystical, they say, as shadows anchored in place.

*Were the shadows to be banished from its corners, the alcove would in that instant
revert to mere void.*
Jun'ichiro Tanizaki, *In Praise of Shadows*

Shadows bending

Shadows bending over whatever's in the way up and over shamelessly,
                distortedly and then

gone again when the wind blows the leaves, when the leaves
falter on their stems—
                that time of year,
a hand on the table, each hour in exact detail, the veins blue

autumn expands over the hedge, clouds seemingly at a remove, pulling
                the immediate rain and weighted darkness over
                the afternoon

particles of fine ash invading what used to be see-through

what on some days one might call *a mood*, a word as imprecise
                as measuring seasons from conception to extinction

similar to a time when scribes copied manuscripts for endless hours of endless tedium,

each hand a mechanical device shadowing
                letters edging towards legible form.

ON THE SIDEWALK

Only a weed—and of the reedy sort out of sidewalks,
unnoticed,   unremarkable but for its shadow cast on the concrete

a thinner than paper-thin puppet caught in a glance,
still,   then only slightly blurred by air—

the beauty of something cast out of mere light and shade
imprinted and unpeeled by finger and thumb,

yet animated by the stirring of air   like strings pulling on the leaves,
a scribble across what is now a moment

extended,   without purpose or connection, the what-for.

PALPABLE OBSCURE

Qualitatively different from darkness on the road and more like fine gray ash

swept from the grate and spilling from the bag I carried it in, out the looser seams

and onto hands, knees, floor, a darkness broken into grainy but archival prints

dissolving in a slippery sheen whereas once it was read as a ghostly sign

adjusting its message on the grate or in the smoky air of sacrifice

whatever's being said or sung piercing this dusty stuff despite the intensity

of *the palpable obscure* that has to be crossed even on the road at night

or in the twilight of history, a darkness taken from the Latin, combining

the abstracted with the concrete, the freefall through obscurity, abyss.

> *who shall tempt with wand'ring feet*
> *The dark unbottom'd infinite Abyss*
> *And through the palpable obscure find out*
> *His uncouth way.*
> *Paradise Lost, book 2*

Flickering forms

It's necessary to begin elsewhere

as with closed eyes we perceive a dark field over which

a curdling luminosity plays

leaving the shutter open for longer than usual

able to record details

unseen by the eye—

her arm up on the back of the couch her hand under her hair

a shadow of a tree on the wall, the fretted edges of a darkening,

the invisible doctored by spirits or gels

the yawning intimacy of erratic light

(self-deceived) (led-astray)

as if following the false light (*ignus fatuus*) down the path of flickering forms

undone by how much and how often we're taken in.

WHERE SHADOWS FALL

Where the shadows fall, they dissolve the impenetrable,

    a wall shudders into windtunnels,

 leaves pulsate against the stacked-up stone
        (rough concrete sewing up the fissures),

the headache as hard as architecture and yet elusive,

wave-like then as a Roman arch monumentally gaping over air

        intangible shadows hunched in corners
dark cochineals

splashing themselves across stucco at the preposterous villa
where walking on tops of shadow trees
        seems a balancing act on someone else's skin.

*The shadow—constitutes the symbolic form of the relationship between the self
and the other.*
        Victor I. Stoichita, *History of the Shadow*

Shadows of night trees
Lyonel Feininger's

Trees were shadows themselves, just themselves against the sleet
           of fog and streetlamp,

Burgkühnauer Alee, powdered with triangular light
branches open in a V as words in mimic: *visible, vacant,*

a face with its pale mask behind the closed curtain of winter

a landscape icing over, out walking in obscurity
somewhat "morbidly sensitive" it was said of him at the Bauhaus

          and so he went at night into the darkness as if the fixity of a face,
the rigor of a practice he hated and the cold itself
could animate shadows in sequenced progression—first one, then the other—

forcing the illusion of movement, as trees (from a foreground pool of black)
          grayed themselves slowly into the distance.

The movements of shadows

Shadows on a tilt and in defiance of obstruction

a backfloat onto black ice and fog
                        a bent sort-of cane walking

in a mimic of trees and fingers splaying

                        upward and intertwined

the shadow graph of a window holding it all in a caged ferocity

in a profusion of cross-hatches

shadows lapping easily over concrete pilings

                        in enviable thoughtlessness and lift.

Philadelphia, Pa 1967 Lee Friedlander

All giant elbows, forcing his way into his own photo,
his shadow overtakes the doorway,

the camera outline lost just above the doorknob
                                 against which a chair is shoved

a torso looming in a shrinking room,
the exact shadow of the inexact, shapeless, insistent—a barrier
to anyone's coming in or out
                                 yet walking seamlessly

through the closed door in a well-worn disguise as oneself
here-again, gone-again, winged elbows of refusal against solidity,

a game repeated over and over testing the tactile world— a tentative
then harder push
                                 as if film could capture that final fade
                                 into a blank wall.

He himself refused any information but the date of when it was made.

The photograph becomes 'surprising' when we do not know why it has been taken.
Roland Barthes

August elegy

Beyond the myopic treeline

                                                    it's the August day of
not being where the chairs are; tomorrow some other chairs,

                                                 the lingering of what was
and of what's to come as if presence and absence were switched,

the chairs a black and white photo over the wooden chest,

a separate causality elucidating the rotted wood, the roof
lasting into an eroded frame of time

                                                 symptomatic of half-light,
a greenish tree cut off by the window frame

and the heart-race of anticipation as to what was to have been an August day,

                                                 each item left-over,

left behind in the coming rain.

ELEGY IN THE MONTHS AFTER

The quiet curries favor with your particular ways as I recall them,
      pulled forward, your absence revising everything after

as cloth might fall into weighted folds, as in the unpainted between the trees
      those raw shapes of exposed canvas

a kind of coming forward marked by formality, your formality
      and the encroachment of the moment before speech.

Afterwards

Afterwards what's left out is what insists:
a swath of tall leaning flowers on the way to somewhere else,
a field lying fallow where the air quickens,

                where a curve arches more fully because of it
and because tomorrow won't be here except as I fold the field as if it were paper
to take with me, it won't be raining, it won't be tilting its light,
it won't be full in the face.

Time always matters, as the woman said, *yesterday I am . . .*
as if it were the present tense of a past time, the immaterial outside of the thing
but the paper isn't what it was like, isn't even what itself was like
before leaving.

                Now the pulsing outline of some backlit shrub
insistent fingers tapping on a distant window.

ELEGY: NIGHT SHADOWS

A cloud moves itself as shadow passing across the earth, as though ceaseless,
as in gestures so associated and so stamped with your presence,
now more than ever—
      as if loss were tactile,
                flat and recurrent as horizons
                the brushed surface of pruned boxwood

dissolving once evening dissolves and windows make themselves a certainty
in the photograph of summer nights with rectangles hung on the yellow wall
behind the square frame of window glass

night shadows forming and dissolving, trailing off
      as the woman in the window memorizes the lines she has to memorize.

In terms of image-repertoire, the Photograph (the one I intend) represents that very
subtle moment when, to tell the truth, I am neither subject nor object but a subject
who feels he is becoming an object: I then experience a micro-version of death (of
parenthesis): I am truly becoming a specter.
    Roland Barthes

Down the hall

Walking in the dark something stirred and I was awake and walking down the hall in a house I know by heart. My arms lifted in case the walls had shifted, but I slipped through the passageways easily and only felt the cloth of my nightclothes brush the side of a door. This time between sleep and wake tastes strongly of the evening before and of the morning to come as the hours shift from deep charcoal to dim near-light. What had the dreaming been and who had been dreaming, I felt for the cup and the water with my hand as the blind measure liquid in a glass.

Down the hall the blind boy slept never moving in the night, never waking until late morning, yet I could feel his body moving in the house, hear his heavy step on the old wooden staircase. The air became denser and more intricately patterned as he moved up and down the stairs and as I stood as a statue, still as possible and then stiller.

My brother-in-law too moved about the house some 500 miles away and dying—down the hallway, his shuffling slippers moving in a slide as if he were fighting against a gravitational pull from behind or as if eager for something up ahead. There were so many shadows whose faces were hidden by the drapery I'd seen on the marble funerary statues of John the Fearless walking along in a formal procession pulling their garments over their eyes. Such projection has become more imminent, more insistent, more often, blindly walking, seeing in the dark.

But as it is oneself seeing oneself—no one else privy to these thoughts— the situation similar to that of the sonnets, self to self (*in me thou seest the twilight of such day*). Still writing is always writing against that day, imaging the person walking the halls, drinking the water, the dense shadows of all in the proximate shadows.

Disappearance

One's own, of course. Bearing advance witness to the missing,
an image in a photo, typing as I am, watching oneself as what,
                                                is not
voyeur of the future in which I am not.

Baudelaire in *Paris Spleen*, "One A.M." released from the tyranny of the human
face, *bathed in shadows*, able to produce a few lines.

     Two days ago the death of the man I married at 22.

An infinite series of . . . . (adjectives),
a remembrance wearing a suit, a wobble, a pile of contact sheets, is not.

     Each as good as any other, missing the point, missing the facts of the case.

Barthes says, unlike photos writing has no evidential force—lacking its photographic
celluloid shape.

Light spilling across the wall flooded his basement. Across the wall
across from fingers I no longer recognize typing a time when I was the age I was.

Light comes in shutters, life-like.

Later on, we say, and mean it. Always on the brink of oneself.

Shadows

who's following, and when one turns
        into the cavity of palpitations

directional as a magnetic dial
        a turning south, turning north
                              it's a swivel in the neck
then spinning on the ball of a left foot
                              rotating into who is it
as if shadow could be voiced (and
off-handedly)

could be what's to be expected, this who's around and to the side
        as in *three were on the road*

                intention seeming a mark of the followed
                        so after a turn

                                    there's a further spin yet

**

a shaded bramble implies   itself

repeated coils generative of burrowing

density of shades, litters of shadows
        overlapped and without material form

each branch laying down its own replica outside the undergrowth what one doesn't think of could take up more hours in the day

a posture seeming to perplex

       plectere to braid   a confusion usually applied
to others (OED: her attitude ~ *es* me)

     the burrowing into

**

so ragged this idea of
    probing whatever it's called, and the breathing into
    and where it's situated

edging out onto the farthest spit of land after which
mudflats underfoot   the slipperiest and most reflective of surfaces

whatever makes for a preference for the tentative,
the pencil mark just barely

the untitled scribble, not a word, a snaky loop, numbers in random progression,
    a question leading up to   a spoke bespeaking other spokes

wheels of the possible in rearrangeable conjunction
in which
       a cloud marked exactly so and she said there were more
in the back meadow, the aftermath of a perished sky

quietude collecting in pools after rain

**

thus with bounty, with scope and proliferation
       beyond the transcribable
           and shelter into which a great number tend,
hidden when needful

the shallows rock-laden and algae-green
             under which fleetingly and uncertainly

with a shallow intake of breath   pausing
belatedly and not unbeknownst, almost unnerving in reticence

as if shadow were the reminder of   what's incalculable
all which is not
and is   as time in its flexible measure allows for

**

shadowing each utterance,
            each word
in revision, as if each time I reached for it, each time
there was a voice, a page, alternates were close at the heels
           grazing the back of, skittering the edges

in someone's voice, a perhaps, a left over
what's always clinging in revisions, shadow to shape
          getting it next to right next time

around the corner of a maze, saying something about the curious
          taking up voice-overs who speak so
in contexts redefined before utterance

wilting in the overly bright sun of the city (azaleas trying out
            their unredeemed lives) as we

search for a shadow under which and into which something might adhere

**

thus into being in shadow and its other
a carving of shapes wrapped around and spoon-shaped
      a graphic stamp, carefully pruned
              or feathered as the wind blows the ends of branches
into shapelessness across the ground—

as if one could glimpse origin hovering on the brink of itself
its use in the coming into shape or falling back into a dissolution

rearrangement
              that curve, an interruption of birds
     deep in the throat   inside hesitancy
        the three of them hold for a time and then deep in the throat
   flutter into and out of

**

by separation, the scissoring off of, what could one call this

often haze more than outline, more than accompaniment

the lag time between one and another

            shading incrementally
catching unaware, smudging chalk marks into disappearance

            threading one blue into one blue
as if thought could be hued

Notes and acknowledgements

"Poetry and Photography and the Transitory"

I've always been drawn to work that juxtaposes the visual and verbal, beginning with my academic work on *ekphrasis* in Shakespeare's plays and continuing into my own writing. We think, perhaps, in snapshots. I'm especially grateful for what photographs have pushed me to see and contemplate: the shapes of shadows and of blank spaces (Sugimoto), reflections (Lee Friedlander) the uncanny nature of ordinary things and their relationships (Atget)—held still for a moment. Photography, film and computer images, screens, and reflections so often dominate the landscape, it is as hard to avoid them as one's distorted image in plateglass. In recent experimental work, poets have used the idea of a frame around description in often startling ways—to create internal friction; to re-contextualize scenes, photographs, and paintings; to combine ordinary "documentary" material with aesthetic analysis, to de-familiarize the familiar and question representation, and to create anew by such juxtaposition.

In his play, Hamlet tries to get to the truth, in this case, the scene of murder of his father and yet, of course, it is missing except in the form of representation: a vivid narrative by the ghost, and in "the Mousetrap scene" a mimed and spoken version. Since all that we try to capture in language is destined to be "merely" a representation, what interests me is the ways in which a writer might make that explicit and suggestive—and photographs stand out clearly as representations of some other reality. We have learned to question them, to recognize angles, cropping, photoshopping, and point of view, yet photographs also carry with them the status/stain of document. This tension mirrors, I think, the ways poetry can simultaneously document scenes, thought processes, images, emotions, and also acknowledge or demonstrate the artificiality of its presentation.

References to photographs become both proofs and failed proofs of what was there. Also, the juxtaposition of photographic images and poetic language itself enacts a kind of failure since a writer can never bring the visual into language and since the alternation of the visual and verbal seems to shatter each, to acknowledge the failure of congruity—even at the moments of greatest success and enrichment. I use references to photographs in poems as proofs and failed proofs of memory, history, documentation. The image stands at an unstable crux and the use of photograph becomes a sign of the omitted or left out. For me, it captures the confusions of memory and history as W.G. Sebald so memorably demonstrates.

Perhaps this is too great a reach, but the dialogue between a photograph and words seems to me analogous to negative capability—putting one in a realm in which the insistence of each unsettles and produces uncertainties. In part this may come simply from placing oneself in the magnetic field of another such that the usual, the habitual, the forces of convention are disturbed. To be a poet is already a dislocation, out of one's time, in league with the dead, in hopes of a world one might believe in, living in language. But another's vision can help, especially, I think, when one surrenders to the "actual world" of things and places and scenes. A lessening of self, one hopes and possibilities of the as yet unrealized, even if each poem—as is too often the case—is only a gesture on my part in this direction.

Photographic images have been allied—by Barthes, Benjamin, Blanchot, and others—with absence and death; they present ghosts and shadows, that which is past. Blanchot speaks of the image as that which is present in its absence, something that appears as something that has disappeared ("Two Versions of the Imaginary"). "Against the grain of a certain faith in the mimetic capacity of photography, the photographic event reproduces, according to its own faithful and rigorous deathbringing manner, the posthumous character of our lived experience," and Walter Benjamin writes, "What we know that we will soon no longer have before us, this is what becomes an image" (Eduardo Cadava, *Words of Light*, 7-8; 11). Not all of us who are drawn inexplicably to photographs— and my interests remain with the black and white ones—are caught up in the experience of not being, but I can't help but think that many writers, even those without any interest in photographs, encounter the uncanny nature of memory and the effort to think the transitory.

In literature, doesn't language itself become entirely image, not a language containing images or putting reality into figures, but its own image, the image of language— and not a language full of imagery—or an imaginary language, a language no one speaks—that is to say, spoken from its own absence—in the same way that the image appears on the absence of the thing, a language that is also addressed to the shadow of events, not to their reality, because of the fact that the words that express them are not signs, but images, images of words and words in which things become images.

Blanchot, "The Essential Solitude"

NOTES
"Illegible," quotation from Baudelaire, "La Soupe et Les Nuages," *Paris Spleen*, trans. Keith Waldrop.
"No sky," for Brenda Hillman and Robert Hass.
"Sugimoto poems," for Courtney Gregg.

"An Illegible Day," for Michelle Lombardini.

"Evidentiary," for Dale Wright.

"Before Leaving," for Bobbi Angell.

"August elegy" and "Elegy: Night Shadows," in memory of Wayne
　　Winterrowd.

"A Kirlian effect": In the 19th c. William Mumler used double printing
　　and exposures to produce spirit photographs; Kirlian refers to
　　a technique to capture the phenomenon of electrical coronal
　　discharges, once believed to be auras or spirits leaving the body.

"Mortified": the quotation by Mac Orlan is cited in *Words of Light*,
　　Eduardo Cadava.

"Remembering beforehand," uses a part of Hamlet's words to the ghost,
　　"Yea, from the table of my memory/ I'll wipe away all trivial fond
　　records."

"Filmic history" refers to the film, *Russian Ark*, Alexander Sokurov.

.

Throughout I have referred mainly to early experimenters and early
modern photographers who photographed and printed in black and
white: Fox Talbot, Eugène Atget, Brassaï, Florence Henri, André
Kertesz, Robert Adams, Hiroshi Sugimoto, Robert Mapplethorpe; and
critical work by Roland Barthes, Charles Baudelaire, Susan Sontag,
Walter Benjamin, Siegfried Kracauer, André Bazin, Maurice Blanchot,
Pierre Mac Orlan, William Fox Talbot, François Brunet, Eduardo
Cadava, Walter Benn Michaels.

Acknowledgements for poems sometimes in earlier versions:

"No Sky" and "A photograph of a side window," from *Partially Kept*,
　　Nightboat 2013. Special thanks to Stephen Motika for permission
　　to reprint these poems.

"Information Systems," *Critical Quarterly*, April, 2009.

"Intimate Portraits," *OR*, April, 2009.

"Flickering Forms," "The factual nature," *OR*, spring 2011.

"The Picture Plane," "Take #2," *Free Verse*, Winter, 2011.

"No sky," "Elegy: a photograph by Robert Adams," *Boston Review*,
    November, 2012.

"Before leaving," *The Laurel Review*, 46. 1, 2012.

"In the photo there is no sky," "The familiar/unfamiliar," *Chicago
    Review*, winter 2013.

"Elegy: Night Shadows," *Denver Quarterly*, Vol. 47, #4, 2013.

"A blurry photograph," Poem-A-Day, Academy of American Poets, July
    9, 2013.

"Poetry, Photography, and the Transitory," *Poetry Northwest*, June,
    2013.

"Evidentiary," "Illegibility," *Iowa Review*, Winter, 2013/14.

"Brassaï," *Critical Quarterly*, April 2014.

"Sugimoto's Seas," *The Laurel Review*, forthcoming.

"The Voice Must Belong To Someone," *50 Favorite US Poets: A Little
    American Anthology of New Writing*, ed. Douglas Messerli, *Green
    Integer*, forthcoming.

Martha Ronk is the author of ten books of poetry, including *Transfer of Qualities* (Omnidawn), long-listed for the National Book Award, etc. *Partially Kept*, (Nightboat Books), *Vertigo* (Coffee House), a National Poetry Series Selection, *In a landscape of having to repeat* (Omnidawn), a PEN/USA best poetry book 2005, and *Why/Why Not* (University of California Press). She has also published a fictional memoir, *Displeasures of the Table*, and a collection of fiction, *Glass Grapes and other stories* (BOA Editions 2008); her poetry is included in the anthologies *Lyric Postmodernisms* (Counterpath Press), *American Hybrid*, (Norton), and *Not For Mothers Only* (Fence). She had residencies at Djerassi and The MacDowell Colony, and taught summer programs at the University of Colorado and Naropa; in 2007 she received an NEA Award. She worked as editor for Littoral Books and *The New Review of Literature*, and is the emeritus Irma and Jay Price Professor of English at Occidental College in Los Angeles where she taught Renaissance literature and creative writing.

Ocular Proof
by Martha Ronk

Cover text set in Adobe Caslon Pro
Interior text set in Adobe Jensen Pro & Adobe Caslon Pro

Cover art © *Shadow of Sign*, Christina Niazian

Cover and interior design by Cassandra Smith

Offset printed in the United States
by Edwards Brothers Malloy, Ann Arbor, Michigan
On 55# Glatfelter B18 Antique
Acid Free Archival Quality Recycled Paper

Publication of this book was made possible in part by gifts from:
The New Place Fund
Robin & Curt Caton

Omnidawn Publishing
Oakland, California
2016

Rusty Morrison & Ken Keegan, senior editors & co-publishers
Gillian Olivia Blythe Hamel, managing editor
Cassandra Smith, poetry editor & book designer
Peter Burghardt, poetry editor & book designer
Sharon Zetter, poetry editor, book designer & development officer
Liza Flum, poetry editor & marketing assistant
Juliana Paslay, fiction editor
Gail Aronson, fiction editor
Kevin Peters, marketing assistant & OmniVerse Lit Scene editor
Skyler Mikelatos, marketing assistant
Sara Burant, administrative assistant
Cameron Stuart, administrative assistant
Josie Gallup, publicity assistant
SD Sumner, copyeditor